Asymmetric Warfare
The Peoples' Guide

John Padbury

TSL Publications

First published in Great Britain in 2024
By TSL Publications, Rickmansworth

Copyright © 2024 John Padbury

ISBN: 978-1-917426-15-2

Battle for Hurungwe
https://www.battleforhurungwe.com/

Contents

Dedication

To those heroes
who fought and died in vain.

Introduction

During the Rhodesian Civil War, I served as an operational Special Branch detective inspector in the British South Africa Police. As an intelligence officer, I worked alongside the Special Air Services (SAS), as well as with other branches of the Special Forces and government armed forces. Initially I was involved in counter-insurgency operations against Chinese-backed insurgents.

From this experience, I learned that traditional counter-insurgency strategies and tactics that fail to include the will and support of the people are futile. I witnessed brave, battle-hardened men fight and die in an unwinnable war. The West's failures in similar war theatres, including Vietnam, Iraq, Afghanistan and, more recently, Africa, epitomise these failures. I then faced Russian-backed insurgents where I learned that it is the people who win revolutionary and conventional wars (*Compare and contrast the strategic theories of Sun Tzu and Von Clausewitz*. [Dr Blick, G., p.10.]). A strategy was devised, in order to mobilise, recruit, train, arm and permanently deploy local residents for the protection of their own communities. The remarkable success of these operations taught me that it is the people who ultimately win revolutionary wars.

We are a world at war politically, econom-ically and actually. Is there a solution and hope for this growing global threat? How do insur-gents operate? Why did Western and Russian counter-revolutionary strategies fail in wars, including the French in Algeria (1954-1962); the Japanese (1944), French (1955) and American (1975) defeats in Vietnam; the Russians in Afghanistan (1979-1989); the American/British intervention in Afghanistan (2001-2014) and Iraq (2003-2011), and the current Russian/ Ukraine War (2022-)? Why are Western and Russian forces continuing to fail in Africa in their fight against radical Islamic insurgents? Conversely, why have outnumbered revolu-tionary forces succeeded (and continue to succeed), against powerfully equipped and well-trained forces? I am not an advocate of war but if the legitimate circumstances dictate, and following in the footsteps of the politi-cians, then fight sensibly. No one goes to war to die (*Battle for Hurungwe*. [BFH],p.457; *Guerrilla Warfare Mao Tse-tung and Che Guevara*. [GW], p.115). As Sun Tzu wisely stated: "The supreme art of war is to subdue the enemy without fighting." He achieved this by the use of subtle, flexible tactics designed to wear down the enemy, while gaining time to develop the capacity to defeat him in orthodox battle or to subject him to political or military pressures aimed at compelling him to seek peace (Dr Blick, G., preamble, Sun Tzu).

Certainly, this is possible, but achieving it demands radical political strategic thinking and planning that embraces the grievances, needs and aspirations (GNA) of the people. Unfortunately, this crucial aspect appears lacking in governments, military dictatorships, global financial powerhouses and corporations, where political agendas and corruption often take precedence, failing to understand or choosing to ignore and/or suppressing the people's grievances, needs and aspirations.

In my book, *Battle for Hurungwe: A Special Branch victory in an unwinnable war* (BFH), I describe in detail the strategies, tactics and military successes and failures of both the insurgents and the government forces. I included the political failures of the minority government to embrace the will of the people, as it remained set on a road to war, chaos, death and destruction. Does this sound familiar? The patterns, principles, strategies and tactics of revolutions are quite similar (Ecclesiastes, Ch. 1 vs 9-11: "...there is no new thing under the sun"). During recent talks and presentations, including some with elements of the United Kingdom's military, it has become evident that our experience needed to be documented in a more precise and strategic manner for ease of reference and distribution. So I present to you *Asymmetric warfare, the people's guide*. In order to gain a full understanding of this guide and our operations during the battle for Hurungwe, I recommend reading the book. A link is provided in the bibliography.

In the main, this guide refers to rural insurgency. While the strategies and tactics are similar for rural and urban revolution, there are subtle differences. These will be expressly noted. I have made reference to Sun Tzu and Carl Von Clausewitz, and for the reader's convenience, quoted Dr Graham Blick's thesis: *Compare and contrast the strategic theories of Sun Tzu and Von Clausewitz*. A link to the thesis is included in the bibliography. As case studies, I have also made reference to the Rhodesian Civil War and the Islamic conflict in the Cabo Delgado Province, Mozambique.

Political Strategic Aim (PSA)

The world is in a state of perpetual political and actual war. Politics involves governing activities, decision-making, negotiations and power dynamics. Power dynamics show how power is distributed, contested and exercised within a political system. Politics should be the bedrock of society, managing resources, conflicts, and collective goals within a society or organisation. Today's politics increasingly forsakes long-standing ethnic, historical, cultural, traditional and social principles in the ruthless and relentless pursuit of power retention. Lies, deceit and corruption are used as "legitimate" tactics, eroding trust, undermining "democracy" and harming societies. This underscores the need for transparency, accountability, ethical leadership and good governance.

"Politics is war without bloodshed and war is politics with bloodshed." (Mao Ze Dong). Simply put, war is a continuation of politics by other means (Von Clausewitz). There has never been a war that did not have a political character. Political wars rage within governments between political parties and nations. A typical example of this is the current Middle East conflict which extends beyond geographical boundaries and involves the vested interests of major countries in endeavouring to secure a political and military solution. Internal and cross-party political strife is evidenced in most governments worldwide. The Russia/Ukraine war serves as a clear example of global politics in action.

Furthermore, Sun Tzu stated that all warfare is based on deception. Since politics is war without bloodshed, political warfare can be inherently rooted in deceit. Consequently, elements of deceit are often found in politics.

Politics is inherent in various aspects of life, including government armed forces, police forces, corporations, businesses, churches, charities, local councils and families. Unresolved political issues and discontent often escalate into war. Politicians then expect their military to gain ascendancy and overpower the enemy, in order for them to achieve their political objectives. Politicians start and politicians end wars. Politics precedes the military and endures throughout the conflict. The principle is that war is political by nature (BFH, p.9; Dr Blick, G., pp.10-11; GW, pp.18-19, 64-67 and 112).

A counter-insurgency war adheres to the Pareto Principle, where 80% of the effort is political and 20% military. This underscores the importance of engaging with politicians, in order to resolve or prevent conflicts, rather than solely focusing on direct combat against "terrorists" (BFH, p.238).

A Political Strategic Aim (PSA) delineates the desired outcome of a political objective, guiding policy decisions and actions to advance agendas, address societal issues, or promote national interests. It is designed to influence public opinion, shape diplomatic relations and pursue long-term political goals domestically and internationally. In warfare, the political strategic aim determines the political aims and objectives and supports the military in achieving them, as both are interdependent.

Military interventions and deployments should not occur until there is a clearly defined and achievable political strategic aim. While this may not always be possible, it could be plausible to achieve 80% of the goal before deployment. However, it is important to recognise that its implementation is always a work in progress (*Twenty-Eight Articles: Fundamentals of Company-level Counterinsurgency* [Kilcullen, D.], no. 9).

The political strategic aim should be rooted in the people's grievances, needs and aspirations. Simultaneously, it should safeguard their ethnicity, history, culture, traditions and societal advancement. This requires the political element to abandon personal, party and corporate allegiances, in order to unite with the people, identify with them and become one with them. Politicians are required to shift from kill-, ego-, political party-, business-, corporate-, pharmaceutical-, global-, and economic-centric agendas (in short, their hidden agendas), and embrace a people-centric agenda. Rather than imposing dictatorial agendas and demanding that people follow their policies, even if well-intentioned, the will of the people is established and implemented. This is a completely different approach. In fact, the will of the people is expressed through the political elements. Furthermore, the political strategic aim requires unity within the political structures: there is no place for division.

Once established, the political strategic aim must be progressively implemented, in order to foster unity among the political and military elements, and civilian population. This embodies a process of aligning with the people, becoming one with them, and opens the door for military intervention by their consensus (BFH, pp.183, 235-239; GW, pp.32-33). This approach stands in contrast to typical deployments aimed at regime-change or supporting threatened or collapsing governments. Such interventions are often driven by personal, global, national or foreign agendas dictated by corporate and political elites, thereby disregarding the will of the people. Any military force engaging insurgents, directly or indirectly, without the people's consent and without evidence of political activity on the ground, risks supporting corrupt political agendas (GW, p.147).

When oppressive governments or revolutionary forces endeavour to maintain their power through the enforcement of both new and established laws against the will of the people, the ensuing discontent signals the fracture of peace. This type of government will increasingly resort to violent oppression of the people, in order to maintain control. Revolutionaries capitalise on, and flourish within, this discontent (*Mozambique is Burning*, pp.17-18, 37-39, 43). Remove the causes and the uprising will cease. Prior to military deployments, political elements must actively engage with the people on the ground, in order to understand and address their grievances, needs and aspirations. Invariably, a social structure exists within which to operate, including traditional tribal structures, local councils and various political, religious and social elements. The crucial aspect is for political elements to actively engage with the people on the ground, endeavouring to build relationships and, where feasible, gaining the endorsement of existing structures (BFH, pp.241, 254, 349). We will go into this in further detail under *Revolutionary principles*.

A typical counter-insurgency political strategic aim involves establishing and progressively addressing the people's grievances, needs and aspirations, and recruiting, training, arming and deploying a people's army. This army establishes a permanent presence, defends the populace and engages the enemy, preparing for or continuing self-government.

Having established that the political elements are active on the ground, building relationships with the people, in order to establish and prioritise the people's will, thereby gaining their consensus to build a people's army, it is time to implement a Military Strategic Aim (MSA). Note that the implementation of a political strategic aim should foster unity among the political, military and civilian sectors, aligning them as a cohesive whole.

It is my contention that a nation should be prepared for civil war, which could erupt at any time. Current international and national situations and developments increasingly point towards the likelihood of civil, regional and international conflict. Oppressive governments, globalisation, denial of freedom of speech, and imposed societal changes are factors that contribute to this growing threat. Rest assured that the enemy is engaged in political, religious and economic warfare, which could escalate into open conflict at any moment (GW, p.155; See *Revolutionary principles*).

If a clear, progressively implemented political strategic aim (essentially, good governance) that is accepted by the majority of the people is in place, there would be no grounds for revolution. Governments and their intelligence agencies should not rely solely on existing structures and methods, as insurgents will be aware of these. Continual change and updating are required to identify and analyse threats. There is a clear distinction and unity between the political and military wings of the revolutionaries (BFH, p.315).

Political Strategic Aim (PSA) summary

- We are a world engaged in perpetual political conflict which frequently (increasingly) escalates into physical war.
- Elements of deceit are often found in politics.
- Lies, deceit and corruption often determine political agendas.
- Political strategic aim needs to be grounded in the people's grievances, needs and aspirations. Such a war is people-centric.
- Political strategic aim must be achievable, and progressively implemented, fostering trust between the political element, people and, when they deploy, the people's army.
- The political element is required to be on the ground, building relationships with the people, understanding their grievances, needs and aspirations, developing trust and also be held to account.
- The political strategic aim must be in place prior to military deployments.
- Attending to the will of the people removes the causes of the uprisings.
- The political element needs to abandon personal, global, political party and corporate allegiances, in order to unite with, identify with, and become one with, the people.
- War is a matter of life and death, allowing no room for ambiguous, empty political promises made merely to gain favour and hold power.

- The political strategic aim should incorporate a withdrawal strategy which includes continuous political liaison at all levels, that is local, national and international (Kilcullen, D., no. 12).
- Consideration and provision should be made with the inevitability of military coups in mind.
- All parties must be committed to achieving the political strategic aim.
- Minority governments failing to attend to the people's grievances, needs and aspirations will increasingly resort to restrictive and oppressive legislation, violent oppression and censorship: rule by fear.
- Nations should be prepared for the outbreak of civil, regional and international war.
- The power lies with the people, but the ruling class does not want this truth to be known.
- There is a clear distinction and unity between the political and military wings of the revolutionaries.

Military Strategic Aim (MSA)

A Military Strategic Aim (MSA) supports and implements the Political Strategic Aim (PSA), and delineates the primary objective of a military operation or campaign, guiding its planning, execution and resources allocation. Situated within broader national security goals, it covers areas such as territorial defence, insurgencies, deterrence, and achieving specific military objectives. Success hinges on a clearly defined and progressively achievable political strategic aim, supported by a flow of information between the people, political bodies and intelligence agencies. The political strategic aim should be known by all military personnel, from the command level to the foot soldier.

In recent years, the downsizing of Western military forces has left them vulnerable to large well-equipped adversaries, as well as to revolutionary forces employing asymmetric warfare strategies. In some instances, capacity-building of friendly armies is seen as a strategic solution, but building armies does not win revolutionary wars: a people's army does. There is a significant difference between capacity-building and building a people's army (See *Operational*). Kills do not win revolutionary wars: the people do. Even in conventional warfare, rearguard, frontline and behind-occupied-enemy-lines operations are significantly bolstered by a people's army employing asymmetric strategies. The people support the stronger presence not the stronger force, as their very existence depends on the military's ability to defend them. This is exemplified by the recent military failures of the Southern African Development Community (SADC) and other private military organisations, including the Russian Wagner Group, in the Cabo Delgado Province, Mozambique (*Mozambique is Burning*, pp.3, 47, 98, 152-153; BFH, pp.143, 181, 235-237). More recently, in 2006, Iranian-backed Hezbollah terrorists, guests of Lebanon and one of the most powerful irregular forces in the world without a country of their own, fought Israel, likewise one of the most effective modern armies in recent years. The end result was a stalemate and asymmetric warfare has flared up again in 2024.

Asymmetric warfare defined
Asymmetric warfare is another type of war: war by guerrillas, subversives, insurgents and assassins; war by ambush instead of by combat; by infiltration instead of aggression, and seeking victory by eroding and exhausting the enemy instead of engaging him. It preys on economic unrest and ethnic and religious conflicts. It is population-centric, the population being the ultimate key to victory for both sides of the conflict. It requires new and different strate-

gies, different sorts of forces and different
types of military and intelligence training.
Politics precedes the military element and the
process of achieving unity between the political and military elements, and the people, is
vital. Asymmetric warfare operates under the
premise that there are no conventional rules to
abide by. Hence the necessity to understand
your enemy and adjust conventional thinking,
strategies and tactics accordingly. The current
strategies employed by Iran in arming and supporting various revolutionary forces worldwide illustrates this definition.

A clear military strategic aim enables the
military to take the initiative and act rather
than react to the enemy. Military operations
focused on reacting to the enemy lacks a clear
political strategic aim and military strategic
aim, and generally does not have the support of
the people. Any military deployment made
without a clearly defined legitimate political
strategic aim and free from corrupt hidden
agendas is, in my opinion, scandalous and
often unlawful. The politicians and military
commanders involved in such a conflict should
be held accountable for the deaths and injuries
sustained by their forces. Furthermore, a kill-
centric war is focused on achieving quick
results, as there are political, economic and
social demands which require limited time
scales, whereas a people-centric war has far less
political, economic and social demands, which

allows for protracted warfare (Dr Blick, G.: Preamble). There is a flow to people-centric warfare: the key is finding the flow (See *Operational*).

Furthermore, a clearly defined and achievable political strategic aim and military strategic aim enhances propaganda and counter-propaganda warfare strategies as the support of the people has already been achieved. Local, national and international media will have difficulties discarding and/or attacking that which the people have put in place.

Military Strategic Aim (MSA) summary

- The military should not deploy until the political strategic aim is established and operational.
- Building armies (capacity-building) does not win revolutionary wars: the people do.
- Kills and imprisonments do not win revolutionary wars: the people do.
- Asymmetric warfare strategies are effective in both counter-revolutionary and conventional warfare.
- Understand the enemy and his ways, but focus on your objectives.
- The military should not deploy in order to support a collapsed or failing government that is not clearly attending to the people's grievances, needs and aspirations. Such a war is kill-centric.
- The military strategic aim supports and implements the political strategic aim.

- The people support the stronger presence, not the stronger force.
- A clear political strategic aim and military strategic aim empowers the military element to take the initiative and act rather than react to their enemy.
- A military strategic aim should include an effective withdrawal strategy with ongoing liaison with counterpart political and military elements.
- The military strategic aim supports and implements the political strategic aim.
- Politicians as well as military commanders should be held accountable for illegal warfare deployments.
- Kill-centric warfare demands quick results, in order to appease political, economic and social demands.
- There is a flow to people-centric (asymmetric) warfare: find it.

The people

The masses have boundless creative power. They can organise themselves and concentrate on places and branches of work where they can give full play to their energy. They can concentrate on production in breadth and depth, and create more and more undertakings for their own well-being... (Mao Ze Dong; Dr Blick, G. pp.9-10). However, despite comprising the majority, they are often indoctrinated to surrender their power to an elite minority. These elites claim to represent and support the people's grievances, needs and aspirations but, in reality, they prioritise their own interests, political party agendas and business or corporate objectives. This alienates them from the people and opens the gates for resistance and/or revolution. The evidence of this is seen in the people's discontent and uprisings (BFH, Chapter 1; *Mozambique is Burning*, pp.17, 27, 31, 38). In fact, it is the people who hold the ground, and the force that controls the people secures it through their support. Furthermore, the elite make every effort to ensure that the people do not realise that they, in fact, hold the power.

Successful counter-revolutionary warfare and conventional warfare, as mentioned earlier, requires the mobilisation of the people, with their consent. Uniting with the people and becoming one with them requires unity between the political and the military elements, and the people. Once united, such an army is formidable and effective (GW, p.155). This approach diverges from traditional counter-revolutionary strategies, many of which focus on a "kills-win-wars" strategy, which has proven ineffective. Short-term victories against insurgents are celebrated by government forces with the catchphrase "we won the battles but lost the war". However, insurgents who permanently occupy the ground celebrate overall victory propagating that they won the battles and defeated the government forces who returned to their bases and airfields, and still hold the ground. It is difficult to argue with that, considering the reality of "who actually holds the ground" and what are the government and/or host forces doing to hold the ground? (BFH, p.189; GW, pp.38, 101; *Chief Makoni and the Shona Rebellion*, p.154).

If "men-in-sandals" can defeat vastly superior military forces by uniting (often through the "barrel of a gun") with the people, it becomes evident that their successful strategies can and should be modified and replicated. Gaining the support of the people is vital for successful counter-revolutionary strategies: after all, the people hold both the power and the ground (Dr Blick, G., pp.7-10; GW, p.19).

The political element is required to work

tirelessly with both the people and the military, in order to ensure that they all understand the political strategic aim. Similarly, the military must unite with the people and earn their support and trust. Once the people feel secure and trust the political leadership, a new understanding of intelligence-gathering operations is achieved. Intelligence is no longer dependent solely on individual informers or sources, or "extracted" through interrogations. Instead, the community freely provides intelligence: it is now their war. However, confidentiality remains an absolute necessity, as elements of the community will continue to support the enemy. Timely response to information passed is essential, as it fosters trust with the people, demonstrating appreciation for both them and the information they provide, as well as the military's professional ability and intent to engage and defeat the enemy. The people's trust should never be broken and is strengthened by progressively addressing their grievances, needs and aspirations. Errors and failures should be quickly acknowledged, addressed and rectified (Dr Blick, G., pp.3-5). Since insurgents make every effort to conceal their identities and operations, information being passed is a clear indication that progress is being made in uniting with the people (BFH, p.330; GW, p.20).

The tragedy of asymmetric warfare is that the people find themselves trapped between two warring parties, with little or no respite. When elephants fight, the grass suffers. It is impossible to counter asymmetric warfare without the support of the people.

The people summary

- The people hold both the power and the ground: they just do not know it.
- The greatest potential for wielding power in warfare resides within the collective unity and strength of the people (Mao Ze Dong).
- Discontent and uprisings signal neglect of the people's grievances, needs and aspirations.
- The people's consent is essential for successful counter-revolutionary strategies.
- Mobilising the masses requires unity among the political, military and civilian elements.
- The people's trust, which should never be broken, is earned through unity with the political and military elements.
- With the consent and support of the people, intelligence flows freely.
- The people are trapped between two warring parties.
- It is impossible to counter or conduct asymmetric warfare without the support of the people.

Communication

Communication is the basis of life and is essential for fostering and developing relationships within and between the political and military elements, and the people. There needs to be unity within the political element, in order to establish, commit to, and progressively implement, the political strategic aim. Thereafter, strong relationships can be built between the political, military, and civilian elements to achieve harmony among all three. This highlights the importance of politicians and the military being fully aligned, or "singing from the same song sheet". Communications and relationships are synonymous. It is the breakdown or misunderstanding of communication that leads to conflict and failure of counter-revolutionary operations.

Early in their operations, insurgents establish good communication channels between their political and military elements, and the people, building strong voluntary or forced relationships with them. Consequently, the people are aware of the insurgents' activities based on their relationships with them. This information is safe as the insurgents rule through fear, often administered through the "barrel of a gun". The degree to which the people are prepared to divulge information regarding the insurgents and their activities defines the degree to which they trust counter-revolution-ary forces. These are life-and-death choices. As far as possible, trust must never be broken and is reinforced by dogmatic adherence to the political strategic aim and military strategic aim.

As counter-insurgency operations begin, one of the primary aims is to gain the trust and confidence of the people who, at that stage, are aligned with the insurgents. Once secured, the people will begin to transfer allegiances and pass intelligence regarding the insurgents' activities. However, the focus of counter-revolutionary forces is to know the enemy but focus on their own objectives. This ensures that they shift from reacting to the insurgents, seize the initiative and progressively implement their political strategic aim (BFH, pp.75, 265, 316; GW, p.71; Kilcullen, D., nos. 26, 28).

The people sit between two opposing forces. It is their relationship with these forces that enables them to pass intelligence from one force to the other. Therefore, there are two achievable objectives: the gathering and dissemination of information. Indirect dialogue targeting the insurgents can be achieved by passing information to and through the people, and observing how the insurgents react to it. This is an important tool in asymmetric warfare. It is accepted that the insurgents are well informed of their enemies' activities, strategies and tactics (BFH, pp.132-133, 244).

Communication summary

- Close communication is required within and between the political and military elements, and the people.
- Harmony is achieved by good communications.
- Trust should never be broken.
- The transfer of intelligence can be a matter of life and death.
- Know the enemy but focus on your objectives.
- Indirect dialogue with insurgents through the conduit of the people is a valuable tool.
- Seize the initiative by acting and not merely reacting to insurgents' actions.

Revolutionary principles

Understanding the patterns of revolutions is crucial for devising effective counter-revolutionary strategies. It can also serve to identify the early stages of discontent and uprisings. The challenge lies in transitioning from kill-, ego-, political party-, business-, corporate-, pharmaceutical-, global-, and economic-centric conflicts to a people-centric approach to warfare. In order to understand revolutionary principles, we will examine those utilised by both insurgents and governments under threat. Systematically integrated into a successful revolution (and counter-revolution) is the pattern of infiltration, indoctrination, isolation and operation. These phases are closely interwoven and difficult to separate, as one phase blends in with the others (GW, pp.18-19).

Infiltration

I define infiltration as "the covert entry into a country, region, organisation or social structure, with the intention of overthrowing the existing government, regime or structure. It involves clandestinely merging in or adopting a disguise to go unnoticed. Insurgents typically operate with a clear united political strategic aim and military strategic aim in mind". Infiltration requires clandestine execution due to the often formidable strength of the existing government's military and intelligence organisations, which would swiftly suppress any early overt actions. In the Rhodesian Civil War (Second Chimurenga), early insurgents attempted to penetrate the country on overt operations before gaining the support of the people. These groups were quickly located and defeated. Subsequently, the insurgents changed strategies and, adopting Mao's strategy "the guerrilla must move amongst the people as a fish swims in the sea", clandestinely infiltrated the country (BFH, pp.67-68 and 196; GW, pp.100, 146).

Typically, insurgents initially infiltrate leadership positions within key political, tribal, local council, religious, spiritual, economic, business and social structures, in order to gain their support (voluntarily or violently), often using fear and sometimes through the "barrel of a gun". Initial emphasis is placed on the spiritual and governing structures. This includes local, provincial, national and political party, and non-government levels. Gaining the consent of these organisations is the cornerstone of the revolution and the key to accessing the people. If the authorities approve, the people follow (BFH, pp.61-62, 314; DGS Report Nr. 467 dated 6-4-1974. Source Portuguese national archives Torre do Tombo FRELIMO, PT/TT/ PIDE/D-A/1/2826-12).

Once an area (cell) is infiltrated, insurgents begin their indoctrination efforts. It is important to note that these initial areas are deliberately small, confined and, therefore, easily contained. The principle is to infiltrate and indoctrinate one small area (cell) at a time, gain their support, control the people and establish an intelligence network before moving on to new territory. This is a slow, methodical, progressive and protracted process which ensures the insurgents occupy and hold the ground with the explicit support of their intelligence networks. Time is not an issue. Success demands the support of the people, and momentum increases as the revolution takes hold (BFH, pp.315-317; GW, pp.49-51, 77).

Generally unaware of the developing crisis, the government and their forces tend to be inactive at this stage. They propagate an "all-is-well" mentality, lulling their supporters into complacency and apathy, a state of mind the government prefers to sustain. This approach reduces opposition and falsely projects that the government has matters in hand. Governments tend to accept any marginal groups, in order to curry favour and retain power, irrespective of the immediate and long-term detrimental consequences to the country. Their focus is on retaining power, rather than addressing the grievances, needs and aspirations of the majority of the people. Absolutes are thrown out of the window (See Phase 1: ZANLA Strategies: BFH, p.69).

Infiltration summary

- The infiltration phase is clandestine, in order to avoid government intelligence agencies and military forces.
- Insurgents initially infiltrate leadership positions within key political, tribal, local council, religious, spiritual, economic, business and social structures, in order to gain their support.
- The primary objective is to secure the consent of the people, voluntarily or violently.
- Success is based on occupying and holding one small area (cell) at a time.
- Governments focusing on accepting marginal groups, in order to retain power, contrary to the traditions, culture and grievances, needs and aspirations of the majority of the people, should be challenged.
- The unsuspecting public are lured into a state of complacency and apathy.
- Initial cells are strategically small and contained. Momentum gathers as the revolution progresses.
- There are no time, economic or political restraints with asymmetric warfare.
- Government intelligence agencies and forces are generally unaware of insurgency activity at the infiltration phase.

Indoctrination
Revolutionary political leadership presents a clearly defined and achievable political strategic aim based on the people's grievances, needs and aspirations, which they "promise" to fulfil. Much emphasis is placed on indoctrinating, training and equipping their forces, in order to promote the message to the people. Having infiltrated an area and following the Pareto Principle, insurgents typically spend about 80% of their time propagating their message among the people. In protracted irregular warfare, there are no fixed time scales, and insurgents or conspirators often "hide", in order to avoid direct confrontation. Dissenters are either turned, beaten or killed. Some insurgents kill, maim, and sexually abuse civilians to exert control. Likewise, some security force members engage in similar actions. The insurgents' intelligence networks play an increasingly significant role in identifying collaborators and controlling the people.

Governments tend to accept marginal groups but, when fractious or violent incidents occur, they isolate and identify offenders within the groups as having been radicalised. Only the radical elements of the marginal groups are presented as a threat to a gullible public who remain complacent, apathetic and ill-informed about the growing threat and focusing instead on a mindset of personal peace and affluence.

During the Rhodesian Civil War, insurgents

initially infiltrated the rural tribal trust lands and gained support from tribal, religious, economic and social authorities, including spirit mediums, chiefs, headmen, kraal heads and businessmen. Those who did not support them were brutally beaten or, if deemed necessary, killed. Moving from kraal to kraal (cell to cell), and gradually expanding their areas of influence, they indoctrinated the people, gained their support, eliminated collaborators and established their own intelligence networks. All insurgent sections had well-trained political commissars who were primarily responsible for this work among the people and within their own forces. They carried out an intense indoctrination campaign and identified with, and promised to address, the people's legitimate grievances, needs and aspirations. Gradually their areas of control increased "under the noses" of government and intelligence agencies, whose sources were either "turned" or eliminated (BFH, pp.67-69; *Mozambique is Burning*, p.43; GW, pp.32-33).

Indoctrination summary

- Revolutionary political leadership has a clearly defined and achievable political strategic aim.
- Insurgents are well-versed in the leadership's political strategic aim
- 80% of insurgency efforts focuses on promoting their political strategic aim.
- Those opposed to the revolution are gener-

ally "turned", beaten or eliminated.
- There are no fixed time scales in insurgency: protracted warfare is a powerful weapon.
- A government's acceptance and defence of a marginal group(s), with a clear revolutionary agenda, is a threat to stability and a road to civil war.
- The role of the political commissar is to indoctrinate his section and the people.
- Governments project that "all is well", lulling the people into a state of complacency and apathy, and focused on personal peace and affluence.

Isolation

Isolation in a revolution is the voluntary or forced transfer of allegiance from one ruling authority to another. It begins when the people voluntarily or by force (often through the "barrel of a gun") transfer their allegiance from the ruling government to the insurgents, who promise to attend to their grievances, needs and aspirations, as they permanently occupy the ground. Awakened to the government's political, social, religious and economic failures and oppression, and noting the military's failure to protect them, the people are "invited" or forced into isolating themselves from government agencies. The insurgents "offer" good governance and permanent protection which is more appealing than occasional police, military or government administrative visits to their territory (*Mozambique is Burning*, p.43). The people are "invited" to attend political meetings and join the revolutionary political parties which are often linked to trade unions in urban areas. They condemn the various forms of opposing rule, such as Western "democracy", autocracy, theocracy, communism, socialism and dictatorship, promising to introduce governance that incorporates the will of the people.

In a rural setting, the breakdown of civil administration through civil disobedience would include the non-co-operation with the police and government agencies, non-payment

of taxes, destruction of, or prevention of atten-
dance to, livestock dips, schools and clinics,
and ensuring that government facilities are
unsafe to staff. The gradual breakdown of law
and order, traditional family, communal and
social order and values, are sure signs of a
brewing revolution.

In religious invasions, the sect's political
strategic aim incorporates a Religious Strategic
Aim (RSA), in order to evangelise, invite or call
the people to join their sect, which they project
as the only "way to God", to live, for peace, love
and good governance. Rather than embrace the
existing culture, they seek to impose their own.
They judge the existing moral fibre of the
incumbent society as uncivilised, barbaric, he-
donistic and immoral, some of which is true.
This justifies an armed insurrection by their
military wing which is deployed with a clear
religious strategic aim that incorporates, justifies and rewards violence.

There is a secondary form of isolation that
takes place as the insurgents tighten their grip
on the communities in what they deem as "liberated areas", where they establish and administer their own rule of law. Their intelligence
operatives, often the youth, now supersedes
traditional authorities, effectively ruling the
people through fear. During the battle for Hurungwe, local judges were appointed by the
insurgents to administer "justice" on alleged
criminals, collaborators, and civil offences

(BFH, p.251). Any alleged breach of security or criminal matters are immediately passed on to the insurgents for action, which is mostly brutal, violent and frequently fatal. In religious invasions, insurgents take care of security breaches, whilst religious leaders become the adjudicators on moral, family, social, dress, ritual and behavioural matters. Orthodox, conformist Christian colonial missionaries, crusades and Islamic operations are good examples of religious insurgencies.

Government responses to these threats vary. It is likely that at this stage it will be alerted to the uprising. When military and police forces are deployed, they continue to expect co-operation from the people. However, without a clearly defined political strategic aim, the government forces will not receive any assistance, as they are alienated from the people. Tribal authorities may well "pretend" to co-operate and offer passive support to government forces but, in reality, they are aligned to the occupying force, by consent or by coercion, and will not volunteer intelligence. Why would they if the government forces do not provide a permanent presence and defend the people? The people support the stronger presence and not the stronger force. Subsequently, the focus of government forces will shift to finding and eliminating the enemy and suppressing the unco-operative people. However, as we have discussed, kills do not win revolutions: the people do (BFH, p.78; GW, p.135).

The voice of opposing thought and opposition political parties and their activities, including public meetings, are often banned and censored, giving rise to further discontent. They are branded as being extreme left or right wing, nationalists, racists, Islamophobic or populists, as the government attempts to rule by fear (BFH, pp.23-24). Pressure is exerted on the administrative authorities, such as the police, civil administration and military elements, in order to pacify the dissidents and enforce the rule-of-law. Significantly and repetitively, threatened governments fail to address the will of the people and make the necessary changes to their policies, which plays into the insurgents' hands. In failing to address the will of the people, the smouldering seeds of discontent germinate, preparing to yield a massive crop. Governing political parties increase their efforts, in order to embrace minority groups, including religious sects, who often disguise and deflect their allegiance to militant insurgents, in order to solicit their support and retain power. As the situation deteriorates and escalates, the government would normally be reluctant to call for regional and/or international assistance, as this would likely reveal their corrupt, racial, tribal and oppressive policies, and potentially invoke a demand for change (*Mozambique is Burning*, p.278; BFH, pp.46, 162-163, 462-463).

Isolation summary

- Isolation is the voluntary or forced transfer of allegiance from one ruling authority to another.
- Isolation feeds on the ruling authorities' failure to attend to the people's grievances, needs and aspirations.
- The pretence of good governance and the promise of permanent protection encourages isolation.
- A government isolated from the people is a lost cause.
- Governments discard absolutes and embrace minority groups, in order to retain power. The will of the majority is abandoned.
- Militant religious insurgents represent religious sects.
- In liberated areas, insurgents establish and administer their rule-of-law.
- The breakdown of law and order, traditional family, communal and social order and values, are sure signs of a brewing revolution.
- Kills, imprisonments and censorship do not win revolutions: the people do.

Operational

With a clear political strategic aim , the people firmly under control and their intelligence networks functioning, the insurgents begin their operations. In the lead-up to this phase, they will have been trained and armed. Selected areas will have been infiltrated, propagated and the people isolated to their cause. Ordnance, including weapons, bullets, hand-grenades, and landmines, will have been portered into the areas and safely cached (BFH, p.69).

Their operational zones will generally be some distance from these safe areas. This serves to protect their supporters and makes it more difficult for the government forces to find them (BFH, pp.72-73; GW, pp.121-122, 134). The strategy of asymmetric warfare is to avoid engaging the enemy unless it is beneficial to the insurgents and on their own terms and conditions. Remember, there are no rules or time limits in this warfare. Protracted warfare is a powerful weapon that strains the government's economy, public and military morale, and stretches their military capacity beyond its limits. Insurgency has two powerful weapons: time and fear, which is brought about by the uncertainty of when, where, why, how, and who will the insurgents attack. An enormous ongoing manpower effort is required to identify and prevent these attacks which drains government coffers. Meanwhile, the insurgents hide, bide their time and create their own strategies

(GW, pp.34, 115 and 118; Dr Blick, G., p.8). Of interest, the estimated cost of the British campaign against insurgents in Malaya (1948-1960), was approximately £450 million. There were about 15,000 insurgents and an estimated 415,000 regular and volunteer government forces. The cost per insurgent was approximately £30,000 in 1960, equivalent to an estimated £800,000 today (GW, p.104). it is questionable whether these costs would be considered acceptable today.

There are some patterns in insurgency that can be learned and utilised against them. These patterns include feeding, socialising, public meetings, intelligence networks, patrols, ambush preferences, landmine procedures, and so on (BFH, pp.67-71, 103-105, 265; GW, pp.35, 112, 146). (See *The People's Army*). There is a timeless, unconventional flow to people-centric asymmetric warfare that flourishes outside of political, social, economic and military constraints and pressures. Conversely, traditional, ego-, political party-, business-, corporate-, and economic-centric counter-revolutionary strategies and tactics face continual political, military, social and economic pressures, in order to destroy the enemy and win the war as rapidly as possible.

Initially, insurgents carry out widespread hit-and-run attacks on selected vulnerable, and isolated civilian, military, political and economic targets. These include remote enemy base camps and patrols, farms, stores, garages, trains, road networks, and so on. High-profile attacks and abductions on international hotels and resorts attracts worldwide media coverage. Landmine campaigns prevent, restrict, deter or harass government forces' movements into and within selected operational areas. They are also used to restrict and control movements of locals. Attacks are spread across a wide area, in order to extend the government forces' manpower, resources and resolve. As the government forces react to the incidents, they are often manoeuvred into vulnerable positions and attacked (BFH,p.134; GW, pp.118 to 119). In this way, the insurgents frustratingly retain the initiative, which has a negative effect on government forces' resolve and morale. They hold the principle that we can find you but you cannot find us. The government forces often vent their frustrations on an uncooperative civilian population, whom they consider the enemy, further damaging their cause. As the revolution gains momentum, attacks spread to larger, well-protected targets and facilities, as well as urban areas.

Typically, government response to insurgency generally begins when the revolution has taken hold and is gaining momentum. Traditional intelligence-driven counter-insurgency operations are implemented with minimal effect, primarily because the people have been isolated from the government and now support the insurgents (BFH, pp.77-79; *Seeking Justice and Freedom* eBook, p.107 of 1058). Intelligence regarding the insurgents' locations, strategies and tactics is withheld for fear of death or violent abuse, if anyone is known or suspected to have passed information to government forces. It is extremely frustrating trying to find and kill an enemy who refuse to engage in direct combat (BFH, pp.69, 78, 123; Dr Blick, G., p.3). Interestingly, insurgents consider "running away" as an offensive strategy (GW, p.20).

Unless there is an innovative achievable political strategic aim in place that incorporates the people's grievances, needs and aspirations and involves the deployment of a people's army, the military are fighting yet another unwinnable war, still believing that winning the battles will win the war.

Governments tend to focus on building the capacity of their armed forces, including the military, police and intelligence agencies, in order to counter the escalating threat and retain power. They project a dedicated, aggressive and no-nonsense stance against the uprising, emphasising their total control of the situation. Laws are amended or introduced, in order to outlaw and curtail insurgents and their activities. Legislation is passed to prosecute their collaborators with sentences ranging from imprisonment to death, despite the government's failure to protect and defend the people (BFH, pp.399-400; *Seeking freedom and*

Justice, eBook, p.108 of 1058). They purport to represent the people, but they do not.

However, politicians neglect the principle that war is politics with bloodshed and that the conflict they have set in motion will eventually require a political solution. Powerful propaganda messages are conveyed to a censored, gullible, complacent and apathetic public, suggesting that "all is well" and that government forces are in control. But, government forces and people operating and living in the operational areas are well aware of the deteriorating situation. Those people living in towns and cities away from the operational areas, and not affected by the war, are lured into this state of complacency. Life carries on as normal.

In the Rhodesian Civil War, this all changed with the advent of a major disaster and escalation of the war. Three major disasters occurred. Insurgents shot down two civilian aircraft, killing 147 persons (there were 8 survivors), and 22 out of 28 oil tanks were destroyed in an attack on the capital city of Salisbury. The people realised that the insurgents were winning the war, could attack ad-lib, and many fled the country as a result. Ironically, the politicians followed the same pattern by staying away from the operational areas, except for infrequent visits to safe bases, but never visited the tribal trust lands, in order to speak to the people. A similar example occurred in March 2021, when Al-Shabib (ISIS) terrorists attacked

Palma, Cabo Delgado, Northern Mozambique, killing 1,190 people. Total Energies (France) were forced to cease their $20 billion gas-extraction development, which drew international attention to the crisis.

Emphasis is placed on enemy kills and minor territorial and battle victories, avoiding acknowledgement of the overall escalating scenario. Consideration is given to regional and international military support in the form of "boots-on-the ground", training and ordnance procurement. If granted, usually this support is used merely to reinforce a collapsing or threatened government that has failed to attend to the people's grievances, needs and aspirations and defend them. Mercenaries and militia are armed but, without the correct political strategic aim in place, these groups are prone to "irregularities" in a similar manner as applied by some special forces (*Mozambique is Burning*, p.98; Dr Blick, G., pp.2-3).

All warfare is brutal, dark, dirty and deadly. Atrocities are committed by both sides. Soldiers and civilians die and are injured. Captures are assassinated or interrogated, beaten and imprisoned. In some instances, captures are "turned" and fight for the opposing side. Civilians are caught between, under threat from, and at the mercy of, the warring parties. Such is war: well, war fought the wrong way. What is the right way and how does the military take the initiative?

Operational summary

- Insurgents engaged in an operational phase is a clear indication that they have infiltrated, indoctrinated and isolated the people to their cause.
- Insurgents' deployment is based on a clear political strategic aim.
- Insurgents only engage the enemy on their own terms and conditions, avoiding direct confrontation with the government forces.
- Time and fear are two powerful weapons of protracted asymmetric warfare.
- There is a timeless, unconventional flow to people-centric asymmetric warfare.
- There are unconventional patterns to asymmetric warfare that are outside of conventional thinking.
- Unrestrained violence is a hallmark of terrorism.
- The insurgents hold the initiative as long as they can force the government forces to react to their actions.
- Arrests and imprisonments do not win urban wars: the people do.
- All warfare is brutal, dark, dirty and deadly.
- Insurgents consider "running away" as an offensive strategy.

The people's army

War is the face of political failure. Political failure occurs when there is a focus on personal, political party, corporate and global agendas, neglecting the need to understand and progressively implement the people's grievances, needs and aspirations. Consequently, the power base of good governance is an inclusive, vibrant and cohesive political structure and process that is obligated to implement the freely expressed will of the people. This is commonly known as winning the battle for the "hearts and minds". But the question is, what are the "hearts and minds" being won to, if the people's grievances, needs and aspirations are not being addressed? The disaster is that in politics, governments purport to listen to the people but in fact follow their own agendas (Read *One Vote Away: Saving the West*).

During the battle for Hurungwe, 12 phases were identified and implemented, in order to achieve political and military victory. This was against all odds and at a time when the Rhodesian Government faced political and military defeat. The National Joint Operations Commanders were so concerned about the dire situation that they approached the British Government, in order to discuss a military coup (BFH, pp.169-171). The Hurungwe was considered a "liberated" area by the insurgents. Government armed forces were attacked regularly, roads were closed because of landmines, buses (which were the main form of transport), were not running, and schools and clinics had been closed by the insurgents. Civil administration and routine police work were virtually non-existent. Rhodesian armed forces were dwindling in number and there were insufficient troops to deploy on counter-revolutionary operations, which were proving increasingly ineffective. Insurgents carried out daily atrocities on the local population, as they ruled through the "barrel of a gun". Murders were a daily occurrence.

I believe that the 12 phases are relevant to establishing, building or developing solid structures relevant to most aspects of life, includeing political elements, local council, routine police work and intelligence operations, corporations, business, social activities, church, charities, and so on. It is important to understand that Western "democracy" is a failed dictatorial form of governance. The process involves electing individuals within a political party who are allegedly aligned with its manifesto. However, once elected, they often pursue agendas influenced by personal, political party-related, global, corporate or business interests, neglecting the people's grievances, needs and aspirations. Yet it is the people who win revolutionary wars and should dictate their destiny, not the global elites (BFH, p.463; *One Vote Away: Saving the West*).

It is important to understand the difference between the traditional army and the people's army. The traditional army recruits, trains and arms a large body of men for land warfare. Recruits are from various parts of the country, grouped together, and are deployed to resolve local and international conflicts, and attend to crises such as floods, earthquakes, and so on. In asymmetric warfare, the traditional army has several weaknesses and limitations, including:

- Government forces are mostly deployed without a clear, achievable political strategic aim and fight an unwinnable war.
- Generally speaking, they are ignorant of the people's history, traditions, culture, language, and so on.
- They are grouped together and deployed to conflict areas which are mostly far from their home regions (BFH,p.452).
- Counter-revolutionary strategies and tactics face continual political, military, social and economic pressures, in order to destroy the enemy and win the war as rapidly as possible.
- Traditional counter-revolutionary strategies are generally and historically unsuccessful.
- Government forces struggle to adjust from conventional to unconventional thinking.
- Government forces are often deployed, in

order to defend a failing government which refuses to attend to the people's grievances, needs and aspirations and/or negotiate a political settlement.

- Government forces face an uphill and frustrating struggle, as they are isolated from the people, and intelligence is hard to glean.
- Building armies (capacity-building) does not win asymmetric warfare: the people do.
- Government forces are trained to close in on and defeat the enemy: a "kills-win-wars strategy".
- Inability to permanently deploy on the ground, in order to defend the people.
- When deployed to assist foreign governments, deployments are limited by political, economic and social restraints.
- Unable to identify with, and become one with, the people.
- Civilians are caught between two warring parties.
- All warfare is brutal, dark, dirty and deadly.
- Legislation, imprisonment and censorship do not win asymmetric wars.

A people's army comprises local residents recruited, trained, armed and permanently deployed in their traditional homes, in order to defend their own people against terrorism. A people's army, local militia and civil defence are synonymous. Some of their benefits include:

- Deployment based on a clear political strategic aim: defend their own people and, in line with the political strategic aim, progressively attend to their grievances, needs and aspirations.
- Success is dependent on unity between the political and military elements, and the people.
- Able to permanently deploy as they are defending, and have the support of, their own people. This support includes intelligence, shelter, protection, and food and supplies.
- Understanding the tribal culture, tradition and language of their own people.
- If able to identify with, and become one with, their own people, intelligence will flow.
- If accepted by the spiritual and political (tribal/cultural) system that holds them accountable for their actions, they are less likely to commit atrocities.
- Progressively isolating the enemy from the people, causing them to increase atrocities, in order to maintain control, simultaneously forcing them to withdraw from the areas that they considered "liberated".

Terrorist operations have several weaknesses which can effectively be countered by a people's army, local militia or civil defence. These include:

- Dependence on the people for supplies, intelligence, social and economic support.

- Generally operating in foreign areas, which allows them to carry out atrocities as they are not connected to the people (no restraints) (BFH, p.68).
- Not governed by the traditional tribal, spiritual and cultural systems, and often impose their own political, social, economic and spiritual governance.
- When not accepted by the people and implementing their own political or religious strategic aim, they rule by fear, violence and other means through the "barrel of a gun".
- The silent voice of the people opposes brutal violence and oppression.
- Unable to, and have no intention of, attending to the people's grievances, needs and aspirations. In most instances, particularly religious uprisings, insurgents have imposed conditions and restrictions that are opposed to the will of the people.

Following are the 12 phases, which were essential, in order to achieve political and military victories during the battle for Hurungwe. I reiterate that these strategies and phases are relevant to the political and military elements, as well as most organisations, including local councils, routine police work and intelligence operations, corporations, business, social activities, churches, charities, and so on. These phases are covered in detail in my book, *Battle for Hurungwe*.

Phase 1:
Gather historical and current political and military intelligence for the operational area.
(BFH, p.184).

Know your people, their origins, culture, traditions, religion and language. Understand their history, including previous social, cultural, political and military conflicts, and their outcomes, as some of these issues may well be ongoing and in need of resolution. In essence, this is a political role required to establish and understand the people's grievances, needs and aspirations. This is a principle of good governance. Sincerity is an important key to this process. It is essential to embrace the people and not condemn them from a position of assumed cultural and/or military superiority: the people see through these insincerities (BFH, pp.238-241; Kilcullen, D., no. 1).

Phase 2:
Establish and develop the political landscape in order to connect with the people.
(BFH, p.238; Kilcullen, D., no. 3).

The political elements are required to operate on the ground, in order to build relationships with the people and understand and, progressively attend to, their grievances, needs and aspirations. This is an essential foundational principle for building a people's army, militia, civil defence, or any intelligence operation for that matter. Trust is based on the empirical evidence of actions following promises. There is simply no place for political garbage and promises made from vain imaginings with the sole intent of deceiving the people and retaining power. In war, these are matters of life and death: political party workers and politicians often die when operating on the ground. I wonder how many politicians would, under these circumstances, venture into the field? (BFH, pp.242-243, 279-281). In order to operate, the political elements will be responsible for gaining approval from the spiritual and tribal leadership or existing governing authorities. This approval opens the door to the people and prepares the way for deployment of the people's army, with their consensus. A flow should develop between the political and military elements, and the people, providing the following benefits:

- The political element is responsible for getting approval from the spiritual and governing authorities (BFH, p.349).
- The aim is to achieve the people's consensus, in order to deploy their own army.
- Once established, information/intelligence flows freely between the political and military elements, and the people.
- Political elements interface between the people and the military, ensuring that the people have a voice. They gather and disseminate intelligence, monitor military op-

erations and actions, and provide feed-back to military command elements.

- In effect, the people become the "eyes and ears" for the political and military command elements.
- Since the people are connected to the insurgents, specific information/intelligence can be targeted to the insurgents, using the people as the conduit.
- The intelligence officer's role shifts to liaising between the political and military elements, rather than engaging directly with the people, in order to gather or extract information. Mature and efficient intelligence officers will always be adjusting their roles and modus operandi.

Phase 3:
Raise the flag in order to create
a permanent visible presence.
(BFH, p.241).

A primary task is to develop a strong political presence and networks, in order to impart a political vision and bring about unity. The strength of the political approach determines the flow of intelligence, and the accuracy of the information corroborates the level of support of the population. These early operations are often required to be clandestine, in order to protect the political element and their supporters. However, operating on a cell-by-cell basis and, as momentum increases, there comes a time when the operation requires exposure (BFH, p.315). (See *Phase 8: Define military strategies and deployments*). A flag symbolises permanent or temporary occupation of a defined area, region or country. It is a visible expression of a shared political vision and portrays political acceptance by the people. In urban areas, a flag is mainly represented by a building. When the ground is permanently occupied by the people's army in rural conflict, territorial gains are marked by the raising of a flag. Normally, this would be in tribal leadership locations, such as chief's and headmen's kraals, schools, business centres, and so on. The flag represents the will of the people, supported by the political element and protected by the people's army. It sends a message to the insurgents and their supporters that the people have re-claimed, occupied and secured their own ground. The challenge is to hold that ground. These "liberated areas" offer:

- A safe place for the people to share their grievances, needs and aspirations.
- A location to gather information from the people.
- A place to disseminate intelligence and information to the people and the enemy.
- A gathering place for refugees and their subsequent relocation to a safe place, normally outside of the operational area. Remember, refugees are generally a source of current, accurate intelligence.

When empires, states, or immigrant populations expand into new territories, building religious structures can signify the cultural, political, and religious influence of that group. (*The Secret Society: Cecil John Rhodes's Plans for a New World Order*, eBook, p.69 of 553).

Phase 4:
Train the People's army
(BFH, p.248).

During the battle for Hurungwe, we initially made the mistake of training men using conventional methods. There was an emphasis on marching, drill, physical fitness, assault courses, and so on. This protracted training had a detrimental effect on the morale of the men who wanted to deploy, defend their families and, when the opportunities arose, attack the enemy. We realised that these elements of training were time-consuming and unnecessary for asymmetric warfare. The people already knew and used most of the skills required in military operations during their daily lives. They knew the territory they lived in and understood how to overcome obstacles, cross rivers, track their livestock, identify and follow spoors, and so on. They understood and respected their tribal systems, customs, and traditions, as well as the spiritual aspects. Communication amongst rural people is complex and extremely efficient: recruits knew the system and how to tap into it. They were connected to their families, relatives and friends, and these relationships would form the basis of their intelligence networks. We devised an intensive 19-day training programme, with an emphasis on weapons training and refining their existing skills, in order to meet the requirements of asymmetric warfare (GW,p.143).

Training, phase 1: Basic drill and weapons training

- Drill relevant to the basic needs of the tasks and weapons.
- Use of, care of, and safety procedures of relevant firearms.
- Specialised weapons training on RPG-7s and mortars.
- Live-firing exercises.

Training, phase 2: Battle procedures and field-craft

Most of these aspects were well known to the recruits, therefore the training was focused on refining their skills and applying them to the military requirement.

- Patrol formations.
- Hand signals.
- Fire-with-movement.
- Ambush and counter-ambush procedures.
- Zigzagging.
- Security of base camps and continual vigilance.
- Camouflage.
- Tracking, back-tracking and knowledge of locals, kraals and terrain, etc.

- Tracking procedures (how to protect the tracker and anticipate enemy positions, etc).
- Political mobilisation of the recruits and strategies, in order to mobilise the masses. This was maintained throughout the training and continued in the field when the sections were deployed.

In modern asymmetric warfare, training should include digital and electronic warfare, as well as up-to-date ground-to-ground and ground-to-air tactics, including drone warfare.

Phase 5:
Understand the enemy
(BFH, p.260; Dr Blick, G., pp.4, 6; Kilcullen, D., no. 2).

The challenge in countering asymmetric warfare is that the enemy compels their opposition to react to their actions, which prevents them from seizing the initiative. The key is to understand your enemy while focussing on, and achieving, your strategic aims and objectives. Act do not react. Hence the absolute necessity of having a clear political strategic aim and an active political element on the ground fostering good relationships with the people. Knowing your enemy would include:

- Understanding their political, philosophical or religious strategic aim which will be centred on the people's grievances, needs and aspirations (BFH, p.68).

- Understanding their strategies and tactics.
- Learn the patterns and principles they are using with regards to ambush procedures, landmine campaigns, attacks on civilian, military, and economic targets and if applicable, digital and electronic warfare.
- Understand how they interact with the people, how they are fed, social functions, and so on.
- Understand how they treat collaborators and captures. One of the reasons for this is to ensure their violent behaviour is not emulated by the people's army.
- Understand how their intelligence operations function, who is involved and how they operate.
- Awareness of those involved in supporting them socially, physically and economically.
- Establishing what level of support they have from the governing and spiritual structures, such as tribal authorities, government, local councils, spirit mediums, churches, mosques, and so on.
- Understanding what ordnance they use, where it is obtained, and where it is cached.

Note that this does not mean the enemies' supporters are arrested or removed. Knowledge is power that can be utilised in due course. Furthermore, it is preferable to "turn" these individuals once operational. A similar approach is taken when dealing with enemy captures. During the battle for Hurungwe, we effectively "turned" captured insurgents and, after an indoctrination programme, integrated them with our forces. The Rhodesian Selous Scouts pseudo-regiment operated effectively with "turned" insurgents. "Turned" insurgents and their collaborators are an excellent source of intelligence (BFH, pp.94-97, 102-109, 339, 406-407; *Mao Ze Dong, Selected Works*, Vol. II,p.53; GW, pp.63, 119-120, 127). Behind the insurgent's mask is a person. Very little escapes the watchful "eyes and ears" of the people.

Phase 6:
Strike the enemy
(BFH, p.271; Dr Blick, G., p.5).

Kills do not win revolutionary wars: the people do. Warfare demands killing the enemy. In asymmetric warfare, the focus is on building the people's army, in order to support and progressively implement the political strategic aim, and defend the people. During the battle for Hurungwe, where insurgents had "liberated" the tribal trust lands, the people were subjected to atrocities, murder and sexual abuse, as the insurgents ruled through the "barrel of a gun". Having identified the people's political strategic aim, and as we gained political momentum in the field and recruited and trained the men, considerable accurate intelligence was volunteered by the people regarding the insurgents' identity, operations and locations. We used maximum available military force in this interim period, in order to eliminate them. Our thinking was that:

- It demonstrated a commitment and ability to engage with and eliminate elements of the enemy, which in turn developed trust with the people.
- Intelligence flowed from the people through the political and military elements and the process built unity and trust between the three: the process of becoming one with the people.
- The insurgents were made aware that their intelligence networks had been penetrated and were forced to adjust strategies, change base camps and relocate arms caches.
- Suspected "sellouts" were sought out, brutally beaten, and often murdered by the insurgents.
- The insurgents were aware that we could strike them at any time or location.
- The message from the political element to the people, and on to the insurgents, was that the people's army is coming. Their rule was being challenged by the people.

The consequence of these strikes was that atrocities on the people inevitably increased. It is important to have as short a delay as possible between striking the enemy and deploying the people's army. As the people's army deployed and in areas that they had not yet occupied, we continued to strike the enemy in order to maintain momentum and protect the people (Dr Blick, G., p.6). Our counter-revolutionary strategy was based on location, isolation and elimination (GW, pp.27, 32).

- *Location*. Identify the location where the insurgents were based at a specific time. It is important to understand how the role of intelligence changed. The local population were fully aware of the insurgent' strategies, tactics and modus operandi. They could pinpoint the location of insurgents at a particular time. Importantly, they were aware of the surrounding terrain of their bush bases and kraals, which they periodically visited. They could identify safe approaches, footpaths, good ambush positions, kraals to avoid, best time to attack based on their known routine, and so on. This information was also familiar to the people's army as they were from the same area, operating in the playgrounds of their youth. All they needed was the actual location of the enemy, in order to formulate an attack based on their intimate knowledge of the area. During the battle for Hurungwe, we used various methods of attack prior to the deployment of the people's army and thereafter in areas that they had not yet occupied. I emphasise that focus was on occupying the ground and defending the people, not on killing the enemy (BFH, pp.103-105, 272, 329; GW, p.115).
- *Isolation*. This was the process of isolating the insurgents from the people by initially

penetrating their intelligence networks, gaining the people's allegiance, permanently occupying the ground and defending them. As the insurgents lost their influence and connection with the people, they had no choice but to leave the area(s).

- *Elimination.* Maximum force should be used to kill the insurgents during initial engagements. It becomes increasingly difficult to find and eliminate them once they realise their intelligence networks have been compromised and that they are losing the people's support (BFH, p.284). Likewise, the people's trust and confidence are gained when they realise you have the capacity and commitment to engage with, and eliminate, the enemy. Enemy kills should be identified by the people as evidence that they are indeed deceased. This is simply to avoid insurgents' propaganda when they are likely to suggest that they had won the battle, eliminated many enemy forces and suffered no casualties. They normally state that those killed in battle have moved to another area. Bodies should be buried in legitimate locations, as documented processes help identify the deceased at the end the war, and takes into consideration traditional, spiritual, ancestral and religious procedure.

Phase 7:
Prepare the people
(BFH, p.314).

It is a fundamental revolutionary principle that the political element precedes the military element, paving the way for military intervention with the people's consensus. This foundation is built through political operations on the ground, developing relationships with the people, and understanding their grievances, needs and aspirations, in order to develop a political strategic aim that is progressively addressed. Information flows freely through communities, both orally and digitally, as a gentle breeze that periodically enflames like wildfire, when important news spreads across the entire area and, with technology, beyond. This is how the intelligence officers' roles shift to liaison between the political and military elements, rather than engaging directly with the people, in order to gather or extract information.

The principles of oral information circulation in rural areas follows established patterns, including:

- There is always a tribal structure in place, such as chiefs, headmen, kraal heads and messengers, which facilitates the distribution and collection of information.
- Children attending schools bring information from their homesteads, circulate it at school, and return with fresh information

to their families. Likewise, their teachers and staff.

- A similar pattern follows people attending clinics, hospitals, missions, churches, social gatherings, including beer parties, weddings, births and deaths, local stores, business centres, bus stops, and the workplace.
- Young boys herding livestock in the fields and mountains gather information regarding enemy operations, including observations posts, foot-and-vehicle patrols, and so on. Likewise, young girls collecting water from nearby wells, boreholes and rivers.
- Information is passed and gathered by people attending government offices and administration services such, as cattle dips, agricultural management programmes, veterinarian visits and judicial courts.
- In certain situations, the police, intelligence agencies and government administration personnel are good sources of information. However, the advent of war changes this dynamic. Where oppressive, dictatorial governments are challenged, these services will naturally be avoided.

The principles of oral information circulation in cities and urban areas follows similar patterns to those in rural areas and will include information circulation at the workplace. The main difference is that urban dwellers are not as socially and communally minded as rural people. There is a greater emphasis on technology, including social media, (Facebook, Tik Tok, Messenger, Twitter, X, WhatsApp and Telegram), internet websites, television and radio.

The main advantages of in-person oral communication includes:

- You know the reliability and identity of the person and the people involved.
- Questionable information is easily sourced and verified.
- Not subject to government technology legislation or censorship.
- Not subject to malfunction or government/enemy hacking.
- Less chance of the information being intercepted by the enemy.

The main disadvantages of in-person oral communication are:

- Possible interception by spies, although this is greatly reduced.
- Loss of control of information spread through "gossip".
- Slow speed of dissemination as technology can reach multiple persons and groups instantaneously.
- Increased risk to personnel who may be targeted or setup.
- Technology can give a wider (state, county, province, national, regional and global, etc). perspective.

The main advantages of digital communica-

tion includes:
- Instantaneous individual or group communication.
- It is not subject to adverse conditions that cause people to isolate, such as storms, government or insurgent-movement restrictions, and warfare in their vicinity.
- Can be encrypted to allow only specific individual access.
- Keep up with modern trends of communication and propaganda-spread, e.g., memes and social media.
- It can be used to identify the locations of participants.

The main disadvantages of digital communication includes:
- Digital warfare could affect communication networks.
- Government or enemy forces can cut, destroy, penetrate or censor communication networks.
- Enemy forces can create false identities, in order to penetrate, intercept, circulate, corrupt, or pass on false information.
- Affordability and poor reception are notable issues in remote rural areas.
- Persons can be tracked and attacked from remote positions without knowing.
- Captured equipment can reveal the identity of individuals within the group and sensitive information.
- Can be weaponised. In September, 2024,

Hezbollah's communications systems were infiltrated by Israeli intelligence and devices in use exploded simultaneously, thereby effectively and severely disrupting full transmissions. Approximately 32 people were killed and a further 3,000 people were injured.

Phase 8:
Define military strategies
and deployments (cell system)
(BFH, p.315).

Development in any form of organisation or institution requires a series of incremental advancements which I refer to as cells. The principle is that, in order to gain ground, a small area needs to be penetrated and held successfully. This is the first and most important cell, and maximum effort is required to penetrate and hold the ground. Failure is not an option, as the whole operation hinges on the success of the first cell. Great care is needed to make the initial deployment a success (Dr Blick, G., pp.10-11; GW, p.80). The process followed in Hurungwe was as follows:

- The political element was hard at work on the ground building relationships with the people, understanding their grievances, needs and aspirations, disseminating the political strategic aim, and gaining the people's consent to recruit, train, arm and deploy their own army, in order to defend

themselves.
- This work was focused on a clearly defined, manageable area for the deployment and occupation by the first sections of the people's army.
- At this stage, information was flowing between the political element and the people; those supporting the enemy were identified.
- Initially, sections would be self-sufficient, but would need to rapidly create local support structures and initiate and execute day-and-night patrol strategies for their own protection and that of the people. This would call for the establishment of their own intelligence networks, which would connect them to their families and the people, and help identify enemy movements.
- The political element's hard work would be rewarded, as the establishment of reliable intelligence networks would now be beneficial. We would deploy and monitor our forces through the "eyes and ears" of the masses. In other words, the people would monitor the activities of their army and feed the information through to the political element.
- At the same time, the traditional way of life was not to be interfered with. Efforts would need to be directed to involvement with the community and the commencement of

political activities in a concerted endeavour to mobilise them.

- This mobilisation of the masses would initially take the form of one-on-one discussions, progressing to kraal meetings, with the aim of holding mass rallies attended by high-ranking political officials, including the prime minister.
- Since our actions and progress would be observed by the people, there would be a need to cement expectations. The presence of the people's army would mark the ongoing fulfilment of the political strategic aim, which would filter throughout Hurungwe.
- Progress in the field is directed by the people. It is important to move at their pace. When the people ask for an aspect of their grievances, needs and aspirations to be addressed, that is the time to act. This approach differs from imposing what government agencies believe should be implemented, even if it is beneficial and well-intentioned. Always move at the pace of the people.

Phase 9:
Deploy, occupy and possess the land
(BFH, p.328).

For our inaugural deployment, we strategised to deploy on positive intelligence, in order to attack and hopefully eliminate some insurgents in the process. After the battle, we would then occupy and hold the ground. This contrasted with typical government armed forces' search-and-destroy, uplift-and-regroup operations.

With the assistance of the airborne, airmobile assault group (Fire Force), we deployed three, ten-man sections in a surge operation into the first cell in a combined attack on the enemy. Two insurgents were eliminated. The people were delighted that their army had permanently deployed, in order to protect them from the violence inflicted by the insurgents (BFH, pp.328-330).

It was vital that sufficient sections were deployed into the first cell, in order to hold the ground against possible enemy attacks. This assured the people that we had the capacity and ability to occupy and hold the ground. Our intention was for the people to regard us as committed, determined and relentless. They needed to view our every action as geared towards their own benefit (Kilcullen, D., no. 15).

Since the sections were deployed into their home areas, they were immediately connected to the people, completing the cycle of unity between the political and military elements, and the people (BFH, p.330; GW, p.127). With the support of the people, the sections had access to immediate essential intelligence regarding the enemy. Furthermore, any intelligence regarding enemy activity and location could now be dealt with by the people's army. Their huge advantage was their local knowledge of the terrain and villages, as they were operating in familiar territory. They could engage the enemy on their own terms, as and when it suited them.

Each section included a political commissar who was linked to the political leadership, and conveyed the political strategic aim to the section and the people within the first cell. The section's medics treated their own men's ailments and injuries, as well as the people's, until such time as we reopened the clinics closed or destroyed by insurgents.

In the meantime, the political element was busy penetrating the next neighbouring cell(s), preparing the people for the arrival of their army. In our initial recruiting campaign, we recruited sufficient men to occupy the first three neighbouring cells. With the first cell occupied and held, we were able to deploy men into the second cell.

Once the people saw the success of their army, we were inundated by requests to deploy into their areas. Recruits literally poured in for training and our operations soon spread across the tribal trust lands (BFH, pp.258-259, 266, 364; Dr Blick, G., p.8). The enemy were engaged and gradually pushed out of the occupied cells as we gained the people's support. Their only response was periodic hit-and-run attacks on our sections from areas we had not yet occupied as they had lost the support of the people. Atrocities on the people increased but we escalated our training and deployments as rapidly as possible, in order to minimise them and protect the people. We trained and suitably armed a specialised combat reconnaissance unit, in order to engage with the enemy on specific missions (BFH,p.350; GW, p.136).

And so the process spread: infiltrate, propagate, isolate (from the enemy and the enemy from the people) and operate. It was remarkable witnessing the power of the people as they embraced the political strategic aim, called for the occupation of their areas, and volunteered to join the people's army. It was like a wind-blown, raging forest fire that leapt across obstacles, often jumping some 200 metres before igniting new areas and periodically changing direction, flowing with the wind. Equally remarkable was witnessing the power of unity between the political and military elements, and the people, and how they became one. Historically, there is little hope of stopping a revolution or counter-revolution once it has survived this phase and acquired the sympathetic support of 15% to 25% of the population (GW, pp.23, 80).

One of the people's important roles was the provision of intelligence regarding both the insurgents and their army's operations. They were the "eyes and ears" that linked the political and military elements, and the people.

They reported progress and problems which helped monitor the men in the field and address issues as they arose. It was for this reason that we chose to integrate captured insurgents into the people's army after an indoctrination programme when possible. Likewise, time was spent with teaching locals our political strategic aim who had been identified as supporting the insurgents. This approach was well received by the tribal elders, spiritual elements, and the people. Of course, there were exceptions. With the first cells occupied, we could progressively attend to the people's grievances, needs and aspirations.

Phase 10:
Restore civil administration
(BFH, p.367).

The people's army's first priority was to occupy and hold the ground, and defend the people. Once achieved, they commenced administering basic medical treatment. Other issues followed, were prioritised and progressively addressed. High on the list was the reopening of roads which the insurgents had closed due to their landmine campaigns. A cell-based system involving the people and the people's army was devised to patrol roads within each cell, identifying landmines to be either removed or detonated (BFH pp.352-353.) Once this was achieved and the buses and civilian vehicles operational, the people wanted their schools reopened which had also been closed by the insurgents. These were progressively and permanently reopened which was a significant achievement, as once reopened it was essential that they remained open. Thereafter, they called for the reopening of their clinics which were permanently reopened. Gradually and progressively the people's grievances, needs and aspirations were attended to and civil administration restored. Military victory should include and support the political element's progressive restoration of civil administration, in order to avoid leaving a vacuum of chaos and disorder to ferment. The people were allowed, and encouraged, to continue with their traditions which had been restricted and, in some cases, banned by the insurgents.

Phase 11:
Expand politically, militarily
and civically
(BFH, p.375).

The initial strategy was to occupy the ground and defend the people on a cell-by-cell basis. Each cell functioned as a complete unit with ongoing political education, intelligence operations, recruiting volunteers for the people's army, and challenging the enemies' supporters. What was significant about this approach was that the military element was not centrally based at a headquarters and deploying on intelligence or reacting to the insurgents' actions, and returning to their bases. The operation was spread across the entire tribal trust lands (operational theatres), as individual units were quite capable of engaging the enemy, defending and propagating the people. Once sufficient ground was occupied and held, it was possible to organise mass rallies to be addressed by senior political leaders. Up to this stage, small political meetings were held on a cell-to-cell basis, often grouping neighbouring cells together. It was time to bring the community together in a show of power and unity. Successful, well-attended, peaceful rallies were held bolstering the people's resolve, confidence, unity and hope. Major political changes were being progressively implemented and envisioned. The people were aware that their grievances, needs and aspirations were being attended to. Massive rallies were held in the capital and larger cities, and attended by people across the nation. Simultaneously, we continued to expand political operations into neighbouring tribal trust lands, towns and villages, preparing the way for the growing people's army.

It was interesting, that as the insurgents lost the people's support and were forced out of the Hurungwe, their only response was infrequent hit-and-run attacks on our sections, and atrocities on the people in areas not yet occupied. They were no longer a force to contend with in the Hurungwe.

Phase 12:
Orchestrate the freedom to vote
(BFH, p.412).

With the political strategic aim in Hurungwe being progressively achieved, it was time to orchestrate the people's freedom to vote on a one-man, one-vote basis. Up to this point, a minority elite had ruled the majority. With national "democratic" elections scheduled, our political wing commenced teaching the people their rights and how to vote, as most had never voted. The number of political rallies increased in size and locations as the people enthusiastically embraced the upcoming elections. On the planned date, the peaceful elections were held and a new government, representing the majority, was ushered in. However, due to international politics, this government was not recognised and the war continued. Despite this, the fact remains that the people's army, against all odds, created and maintained a safe environment for the people to live in and vote in a free-and-fair election.

About "democracy"

The South African foreign minister, Pik Botha (1977-1994), correctly summed up the current state of affairs regarding "democracy" when he said: "Politicians suffer from power hunger, the need to dominate. The bloody job boils down to one thing: a central authority that has to be formed — a state under a head. Everything ultimately depends on dictatorship, even a parliament. In the end the voice of the people counts for nothing, the politicians do whatever they like — whether it is Bush or Thatcher or Hitler. Only some of them don't commit such a terrible number of murders. But nobody really follows Christ's doctrine of love" (BFH p.463). Once elected, the ruling political party and its politicians pursue global, corporate, and their own collective and individual agendas.

The principle of Western "democracy" is that people are free to vote for the political candidates and party of their choice. Politicians aim to capture the imagination and votes of the electorate. However, once elected, due to corruption, deceit, hidden agendas and hubris, these politicians often capture the state. This is known as state-capture: when the state exists to serve the politicians and their hidden agendas rather than the people. Democracy cannot survive without transparency. State institutions, including the police, judiciary, armed forces and intelligence agencies, claim to defend both the state and the people. But, if the state is captured, who are these institutions really protecting: the people or the state? And, the wars being fought: are they for king and country, the state, or for the defence of the people? In 1902, Viscount Alfred Milner (1854–1925, a British statesman, colonial administrator, and influential figure in the British Empire), was sceptical of democratic government, believing that a dedicated, hand-picked elite was better suited to manage a nation's affairs (*The Secret Society: Cecil John Rhodes's Plans for a New Word Order*).

In his book, *One Vote Away: Saving the West*, Neil Petrie makes it clear: "that the way forward is to adopt the Swiss semi-direct form of "democracy", where the people govern and the politicians administer. The Swiss have political parties but the MPs only work around 12 weeks a year, the rest of the time most of them have other jobs. This means that they are part of society and not separate from it, and that their direct costs are negligible. Swiss voters vote four times a year, mainly on referendums which have been called by the people, not the politicians. Sometimes these are mandatory votes on constitutional changes, others are on amending or voting down a new law from parliament, and other times they are initiatives put forward by the public. The oversight that the public have ensures that corruption, waste and mismanagement are negligible, and that decisions are generally made lower down the system and more locally than in other nations. In the end, it is always the people who decide what the laws are that they live by. A real "democracy", unlike our elective oligarchies (representative "democracies") (Neil Petrie).

A way forward needs to be found that allows the expression and progressive realisation of the people's grievances, needs and aspirations through a political system that is committed and dedicated to good governance. The present system of "democracy" is little more than a mechanism for electing elites (often corrupt, deceptive and privileged) set on their own, or global, corporate or party agendas. The people, who have been deceived for so long, and fought and died for the "system", hold the power. Direct "democracy" offers the foundations for a just and equitable society. It is time to embrace change. It is the people's time.

Conclusion

The people's army in Hurungwe were self-sufficient and unaccompanied by military personnel. They were a visible force, suitably armed and prepared for confrontation with the enemy, and inextricably connected to the people. In 11 months, the political and military elements, and the people, achieved the following:

- Recruited, trained, armed and permanently deployed 762 local men to defend their own people in the Hurungwe Tribal Trust Lands.
- Progressively attended to the people's grievances, needs and aspirations and reintroduced civil administration.
- Lifted 56 landmines with the support of the people and reinstated the rural bus service previously stopped by the insurgents.
- Permanently reopened 24 schools previously closed by the insurgents.
- Reopened clinics and cattle dips.
- Isolated the insurgents from the people and forced them to withdraw from Hurungwe and periodically engaged them in battle.
- Created a safe environment for the people in which to live in and vote.
- Three members of the people's army were killed in action (R.I.P.).

However, this success could not have been

achieved without:

- A clearly defined and progressively implemented political strategic aim based on the
people's grievances, needs and aspirations.
- A clearly defined military strategic aim supported and reinforced by the political strategic aim.
- The active involvement of the political elements on the ground. They had to be seen
to honour their word and be committed to
the successful outcome, despite inevitable
periodic setbacks. Understanding that:
  i.   The people, and not politicians, hold the
       power.
  ii. The people win revolutionary wars.
  iii. Kills, imprisonments and censorship do
       not win revolutions: the people do.
- Assistance from special forces' units of the
government armed forces trained to attack
and eliminate the enemy. Once established,
the combat reconnaissance unit took over
this role.
- Most importantly, the support of the people served as the cornerstone for success,
ensuring legitimacy, resilience and sustained momentum in a life-and-death struggle.

Commeth the hour

Commeth the people

Bibliography

Blick, Dr G.: *Compare and contrast the strategic theories of Sun Tzu and Von Clausewitz*: https://www.battleforhurungwe. com/post/strategic-theories-of-sun-tzu-and-von-clausewitz.

Kilcullen, D.: *Twenty-Eight Articles: Fundamentals of Company-level Counter-insurgency*: https://www.armyupress.army.mil/Portals/7/PDF-UA-docs/Kilcullen-May-June-2006-UA.pdf.

Ndlovu, V.: *Seeking Justice and Freedom (loyal but not docile)*: Michael Terence Publishing, 2021.

Padbury, J.: *Battle for Hurungwe: A Special Branch victory in an unwinnable war*: TSL Publications, 2022. https://www.battleforhur ungwe.com/.

Petrie, N.: *One Vote Away: Saving the West*: Independently published, 2023.

Rhodes, C.J.: *The Secret Society: Cecil John Rhodes's Plans for a New Word Order*: Penguin Books, 2015, eBook.

Tanser, T., *Chief Makoni and the Shona Rebellion*: Heritage of Zimbabwe Publi-cation 10 (1991).

Tse-Tung, M. and Guevara, C.: *Guerrilla Warfare by Mao Tse-Tung and by Che Guevara*: Cassell & Company, 1961.

Vambe, M., Saurombe, A., Lazaro, J. and Ruhanya, P.: *Mozambique is burning: Islamic Insurgency in Cabo Delgado*: Beaver Press, 2022; African Institute for Culture, Peace, Dialogue & Tolerance Studies (Harare).

Recommended reading

Taber, R.: *War of the Flea, the classic study of guerrilla warfare*: Brassey's Inc., 2002.

Tsu, Sun.: *Art of War*: Penguin Classics, 1st ed. 29 May 2008.

Zedong, M.: *Quotations from Chairman Mao Tsetung: (The Little Red Book)*: Foreign Languages Press, Peking, 1976.